SILK FLORALS FOR THE HOLIDAYS

✦

CELE KAHLE

Silk Florals

FOR THE HOLIDAYS

✦

CELE KAHLE

NORTH LIGHT BOOKS

www.artistsnetwork.com

cincinnati, ohio

CELE KAHLE HAS BEEN A FLORAL DESIGNER FOR SEVEN- *about the author*

TEEN YEARS, AND IS THE AUTHOR OF *FABULOUS SILK FLORALS FOR THE HOME*. SPECIALIZING IN SILK FLOWER ARRANG-

ING, SHE CURRENTLY WORKS AS A DESIGN CONSULTANT, CREATING CUSTOM FLORAL DECORATIONS FOR PRIVATE

HOMES. A SELF-TAUGHT FLORAL DESIGNER, CELE LOVES TO SHARE HER LOVE OF FLOWER

ARRANGING WITH OTHERS. SHE LIVES WITH HER HUSBAND, KEN, AND THREE CHILDREN,

SETH, STEPHANIE AND HAILEY, IN COLDWATER, OHIO.

Other fine North Light Books are available from your local bookstore or art supply store or direct from the publisher.

05 04 03 02   5 4 3 2 1

Library of Congress Cataloging-in-Publication Data
Kahle, Cele
    Silk florals for the holidays / by Cele Kahle.-- 1st ed.
        p. cm.
    ISBN 1-58180-259-5 (alk. paper)
    1. Silk flower arrangement. 2. Holiday decorations. I. Title.

SB449.3.S44K35 2002
745.92--dc21

                    2002016612

EDITOR: Catherine Cochran
DESIGNER: Andrea Short
PRODUCTION COORDINATOR: Sara Dumford
PRODUCTION ARTIST: Cheryl VanDeMotter
PHOTOGRAPHERS: Christine Polomsky and Tim Grondin

acknowledgments

I AM EXTREMELY THANKFUL TO GOD FOR BLESSING ME WITH THE GIFT OF CREATIVITY THAT I CAN SHARE WITH OTHERS. SPECIAL THANKS TO MY HUSBAND, KEN, FOR HIS LOVE AND PATIENCE. I AM GRATEFUL FOR HIS ENCOURAGEMENT WHILE MAKING THIS BOOK. MANY THANKS TO MY FAMILY AND FRIENDS, FOR SUPPORTING AND ASKING ME TO DECORATE THEIR HOMES AND BUSINESSES WITH FLORAL DESIGNS THROUGHOUT THE YEARS. THANKS TO MY MOM, CECELIA, WHOM I WAS NAMED AFTER, FOR NOT ONLY PASSING ON HER GIFT OF CREATIVITY TO ME, BUT ALSO FOR ENCOURAGING HER SIXTEEN CHILDREN TO WORK HARD. THANK YOU TO MY SISTER, WANNITTA, FOR NOT ONLY GETTING ME STARTED IN THE FLORAL DESIGN BUSINESS BUT FOR HER CONSTANT SUPPORT AND LOVE. THANKS TO MY SISTER-IN-LAW, KAREN, WHO APPRECIATED MY TALENT AND INTRODUCED ME TO THE F&W PUBLICATIONS STAFF. A WARM THANKS TO MY FRIENDS AT F&W PUBLICATIONS, TRICIA WADDELL, MY EDITOR CATHERINE COCHRAN AND MY PHOTOGRAPHER CHRISTINE POLOMSKY. THEIR HELP IN MAKING THIS BOOK WAS INVALUABLE.

✦

I DEDICATE THIS BOOK TO MY HUSBAND, KEN, AND OUR CHILDREN, SETH, STEPHANIE AND HAILEY, FOR THEIR LOVE AND FOR INSPIRING ME EVERY DAY.

✦ *Projects*

✦ INTRODUCTION

THIS BOOK IS FILLED WITH BEAUTIFUL HOLIDAY ARRANGEMENTS THAT ANYONE CAN CREATE

AND ENJOY. I WILL SHOW YOU HOW TO CREATE FESTIVE ARRANGEMENTS FOR A VARIETY OF

HOLIDAYS, FROM A BLOOMING EASTER WREATH

I love spending the holidays with
family and friends—and what's more,
I love decorating for them!

AND A FOURTH OF JULY BASKET TO A HALLOWEEN

JACK O' LANTERN AND A CHRISTMAS TOPIARY.

EACH HOLIDAY BECOMES SPECIAL WITH UNIQUE

FLOWER ARRANGEMENTS YOU CAN MAKE THROUGHOUT THE YEAR.

HOLIDAYS ARE A TIME TO ENJOY AND CELEBRATE WITH YOUR LOVED ONES. IT IS

ALSO NO SECRET THAT THEY CAN BE VERY STRESSFUL WITH ALL OF THE DECORATING AND

ENTERTAINING! THIS BOOK CONTAINS A WIDE VARIETY OF FLOWER ARRANGEMENTS FROM

CENTERPIECES AND WREATHS TO TOPIARIES AND SWAGS, BUT THEY ALL HAVE ONE THING IN

COMMON: CLEAR, EASY-TO-FOLLOW INSTRUCTIONS THAT GUARANTEE SUCCESS. YOU WILL

AMAZE YOURSELF BY CREATING THESE FESTIVE DESIGNS IN ONLY AN HOUR OR TWO, EVEN IF

YOU HAVE LITTLE OR NO EXPERIENCE. DON'T BE AFRAID TO PICK UP THIS BOOK AND BE CRE-

ATIVE. IN NO TIME, YOU WILL DISCOVER YOUR OWN HOLIDAY FLORAL DESIGN STYLE AND

IMPRESS YOUR FAMILY AND FRIENDS!

CELE KAHLE

◆ Getting Started

EVEN IF YOU HAVE LITTLE OR NO EXPERIENCE, YOU CAN EASILY CREATE STUNNING FLORAL ARRANGEMENTS IN NO TIME. WHETHER IT IS SELECTING THE BEST FLOWERS FOR THE SEASON AND HOLIDAY OR CHOOSING THE BEST CONTAINER, THIS SECTION WILL HELP YOU WITH THE BASICS TO ACCESSORIZE YOUR HOLIDAY DÉCOR ALL YEAR ROUND.

HOLIDAYS & FLOWERS

The focus of each holiday should be celebrating with your family and friends. It should not be a time for stress, worry or headaches. Flowers have a calming effect on people, so let them help you relax during the holidays! Flowers are also a simple way to completely transform the look of a room. The most important thing to remember is that your holiday décor is a reflection of you and what is important to you. Keep these floral arranging basics in mind as you develop your own holiday floral style.

✦ FLOWER SELECTION

There is a wide range of artificial flowers available for each season. The best time to select artificial flowers for a specific holiday is just prior to the holiday itself. Many retail stores make these flowers available up to three months in advance. Look for silk flowers with wired stems, petals and leaves, so you can individually bend and reshape each flower to look natural. Many spring, summer and fall flowers look so realistic, you often have to touch them to tell if they are real. Unnaturally colored flowers will make your arrangements look fake and dated. I like to add silver and gold accents to my holiday arrangements, especially for Christmas and New Year's. Gold accents give the arrangement a magical look, perfect for setting the holiday mood.

✦ PROPORTION

The best way to select flowers for an arrangement is to make a bouquet in your hand, checking the size and color relationships of the flowers. When choosing the size and proportion of the flowers, also consider the size of the container and the style of the décor. I personally choose large flowers in many of my floral arrangements. Larger flowers give a more dramatic look; they also take up more space in the arrangement, so you will need fewer flowers. Most larger flowers are wired, which allows you to bend and shape them to give a more natural appearance.

In many of the arrangements in this book, I use flower stems with multiple blooms per stem. If you cannot find stems with multiple blooms, substitute by taping two individual stems together or put the two stems close to one another in the arrangement.

When selecting flowers, gather a bouquet in your hands to help you determine the appropriate color and proportion.

✦ Color

When choosing flowers for your holiday arrangements, choose seasonally appropriate colors that remind you of the holiday and complement the décor of your room. In the spring and summer, use bright and colorful flowers. In autumn, choose more golden tones. The colors in your arrangement should depend on the tones you already have in your home décor or colors specific to the holiday itself. Choosing colors for the Christmas season can be the most difficult. For instance, if you like the traditional red for the holidays, but have burgundy or mauve for your décor, you may still use red. However, you may want to try burgundy in the arrangement as a unique alternative. Select the colors that you feel most comfortable with.

✦ Silk Foliage, Fruits & Berries

Artificial foliage is available in a variety of shapes and colors. Silk greenery is not only available in different shades of green, but also in different shades for each season. In the spring and summer, greenery mixed with different shades of pink and lavender is very popular. In the autumn, foliage such as faded leaves is available. During the Christmas season, multicolored greeneries are available with gold and silver glitter accents. If the greenery is not glittered and

you would like the festive look, just spray your greenery with silver or gold glitter spray paint. As you will see in the projects, I often mix more than one type of greenery in an arrangement. Mixing greeneries that complement one another is a great way to add color and softness to your arrangement.

Artificial berries, fruits and vegetables are available in many materials, such as latex, papier-mâché, plastic and microbeaded. During Christmastime especially, there are glittered or frosted gold and silver fruits and berries available. You will find them in clusters, attached to vines and as individual pieces. Use them to add color, drama and texture to your arrangement. They are a great alternative to an all-flower arrangement.

✦ Choosing Containers

Containers are as important to the total holiday design as the flowers themselves. When choosing a container, first consider the holiday and the overall feel of the arrangement. For instance, for the Fourth of July Basket I wanted to create a summertime celebration, so I chose to use a picnic basket. For the Sleigh & Candle Centerpiece, I chose a miniature sleigh as the container.

It is also important to remember that the container serves a very functional purpose. Containers vary in height and size, depend-

Silk foliage, leaves and berries come in a wide array of colors and styles.

ing on their intended use. Low containers are ideal on a dining room table, while taller vases create a dramatic display in a doorway. Keep in mind decorating basics such as color, texture, size and location, so both the flowers and the container complement your total decorating scheme.

✦ Ribbon

To enhance an already dazzling arrangement, add a decorative bow using some festive ribbon. There is an enormous selection of ribbon available at craft, fabric, and discount stores. Personally, I prefer wide wired ribbon with floral arrangements, because it holds the shape of the bow and is more durable. You can find ribbon to match specific holidays, especially during Christmas, Thanksgiving, Halloween or the Fourth of July. For Easter and other springtime holidays, choose ribbons that have pastel colors, such as a sheer plaid ribbon with pinks, yellows and greens. During the autumn and winter holidays, you may want to use velvet or another heavier ribbon. No matter what the season or holiday, ribbon adds a finished touch to your arrangements. ✦

When choosing a container, consider the height, weight and proportions of the floral arrangement, as well as the overall theme of the holiday.

✦ Basic Tools & Techniques

NOTHING IS MORE IMPORTANT THAN HAVING THE RIGHT TOOLS AND MATERIALS TO CREATE HOLIDAY ARRANGEMENTS QUICKLY AND EASILY. ONCE YOU LEARN BASIC ARRANGING TECHNIQUES, YOU CAN START CREATING STUNNING ARRANGEMENTS LIKE A PRO. THIS SECTION DETAILS THE BASIC TOOLS AND TECHNIQUES YOU NEED TO CREATE ANY ARRANGEMENT IN THIS BOOK.

BASIC TOOLS & SUPPLIES

Most craft stores carry the basic flower-arranging tools and materials you will need to create silk arrangements. You can also buy materials from your local florist.

floral sheet foam: Floral foam is used to secure flower stems in an arrangement. I used 2" (5cm) thick green foam in all of the projects. I prefer sheet foam over foam blocks because it is more dense and firm, so stems are held more securely.

floral pick extenders: Floral picks come in several sizes and are useful in extending stem lengths and securing bows. I use 4" (10cm) wooden floral picks with wire for all of the arrangements in this book.

floral tape: Used to wrap stems with floral picks or to bind flower stems together, floral tape is a self-sealing tape that is activated by the heat from your fingers. Floral tape is

available in different colors. I used dark green for all the projects in this book.

floral adhesive tape: Floral adhesive tape such as Cling is a sticky claylike material used to secure items in your arrangement. Use floral adhesive tape to attach foam pieces together, secure foam inside a container or secure a figurine to foam.

floral wire: Floral wire comes in different weights or gauges. For the arrangements in this book, you will need 22-gauge wire. I often use floral wire to secure bows in the arrangements.

greening pins: Sometimes called S–pins or floral pins, they are used to secure moss or other floral materials to foam.

wire cutters: You need easy–to–handle wire cutters to cut thin–stemmed silk flower stems

or dried material. For heavier stems, a stronger pair may be necessary.

serrated knife: Use a serrated knife to cut floral sheet foam for silk arrangements.

glue gun: A glue gun can be used for many different projects. I prefer a glue gun that has several heat settings, but I generally use the lowest setting. In this book I used a glue gun mainly to secure flowers and floral picks to wreaths and accessories.

glitter floral spray: Glitter floral sprays have bright metallic flecks to brighten and enhance silk flowers. I use Decorating Magic Spray Glitter, which is specifically designed for floral materials.

gold aerosol floral spray paint: Gold floral spray paint is wonderful for accenting baskets, dried floral materials, silk flowers and floral accessories. For the projects in this book, I used 24 Karat Gold by Floralife.

snow spray: Snow spray can be used on silk and fresh flowers alike to give the project a snowy appearance.

plastic candle holder: Plastic candle holders come in several sizes to secure a candle safely in an arrangement. The bottom of the holder has a stake so it fits securely in foam.

12

BASIC TECHNIQUES

These are the basic techniques you will use over and over again to complete the arrangements in this book. From stem wrapping to bow making, these techniques will make your arrangements look as if they were done by a professional.

✦ PREPARING YOUR CONTAINER WITH FOAM

Depending on the size and shape of your container, there are two ways you can prepare it with foam. The first technique works best for a container that is not very deep and does not have a lip around the edge. To prepare your container using this technique, you need a ruler, serrated knife, greening pins, floral adhesive tape and floral foam. In this technique, and for most of the projects in this book, I stack two pieces of foam so that they sit at least 1"–2" (3cm–5cm) above the container.

The second technique is used when you have a round vase or irregularly shaped container. Basically, you make an imprint of the opening of the vase in the foam and then cut the foam to fit inside. Line the lip of the vase with floral adhesive and attach the foam, leaving 1"–2" (3cm–5cm) above the rim of the container.

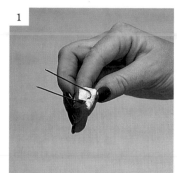

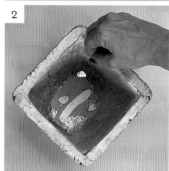

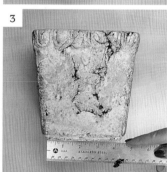

1. Take a 2" (5cm) strip of floral adhesive and wrap it around the top of a greening pin. The number of pins you will need depends on the size of the container opening. For example, if I had a 9" (23cm) diameter container, I would use about six greening pins.

2. Press the greening pins with floral adhesive tape to the bottom of the container. Put a strip of floral adhesive tape in the center of your container. This will make the foam secure inside the container.

3. Measure the length and width of the base of your container, then cut a piece of foam ½" (1cm) smaller than these measurements.

4. Push the foam down firmly into the bowl into the greening pins and adhesive at the bottom of the container.

5. Put two long strips of floral adhesive on top of the foam in the container.

6. Measure the top opening of the container, and cut another piece of foam ½" (1cm) smaller to fit inside the container. Press it down firmly on top of the first piece of foam.

13

1. *Press the vase into the foam to make an imprint of the vase opening.*

2. *Use the imprint as a guide for cutting the foam with a serrated knife. Shave the sides at an angle to fit snugly inside the vase.*

3. *Put floral adhesive tape around the inside lip of the vase.*

4. *Press the foam into the vase so it fits snugly, leaving 1"–2" (3cm–5cm) of foam above the rim of the vase.*

14

opening silk flowers

✦ OPENING SILK FLOWERS

When packaged, silk flowers are often folded and flattened, but they can be easily molded and brought to life. Here's an easy way to bring out the natural beauty of silk flowers.

1. *Most silk flower stems are folded up like this rose stem when you buy them.*

2. *Begin unfolding the flower from the bottom. Start with the leaves and work your way up the stem. When opening the flowers, arrange the petals as naturally as you can.*

3. *Your silk flower takes on a fresh look when unfolded and molded by your hands. To keep your silk flowers and foliage looking fresh and free of dust, periodically wipe them off with a damp cloth or gently blow–dry the dust off the surface.*

✦ USING FLORAL PICK EXTENDERS

Wooden floral picks with wire extenders are used for several reasons: to make a flower stem longer, to make a weak stem stronger, and to secure and attach bows. Although they come in several lengths, I generally use the 4" (10cm) size. If you need a shorter length, cut it to the size you prefer. If you need more length, purchase longer floral pick extenders or use a wired stem that has been cut from a flower. (Many flowers come with extra-long stems, so when I cut them off, I keep the extra stems in case I need a long extender.) To extend silk flower stems, use floral tape to securely attach the floral picks with wire extenders. This technique also works for attaching cut wire stems for extra-long extenders.

1. *Take your wooden floral pick with wire and lay it next to your flower stem, extending the pick 1½" (4cm) above the end of the stem. Wrap the wire securely down the stem.*

2. *Begin wrapping the stem with floral tape, starting just above the floral pick. Floral tape does not have a right or wrong side. It becomes tacky and adheres to itself when you start working with it. Hold the flower with one hand and the tape in the other, stretching and working the tape downward. The tape should be snug, overlapping on its way down the stem.*

3. *Be sure to smooth the tape with your fingers to make it secure. This is how the finished wrapped stem looks.*

✦ Bow Making

You will find that nearly every project in this book is finished with a bow. Ribbons can enhance the arrangement and complement the flowers. I recommend using wired ribbon. It not only makes the nicest bows, but it is also easiest to work with. There are so many beautiful ribbons available, you will enjoy the extra touch they add to your holiday arrangements.

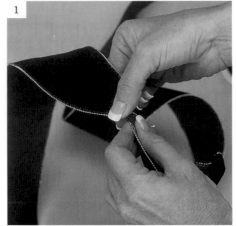

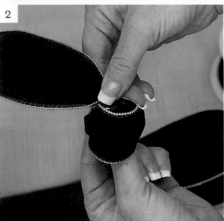

1. *Begin by pinching the ribbon between your fingers approximately 5" (13cm) from the end.*

2. *Form the "knot" of the bow by making a small loop with the 5" (13cm) of ribbon.*

3. *Hold the "knot" of the bow and twist the ribbon. Make a larger loop, which will become the start of the actual bow. The size of the loop will determine the width of your bow. As you complete the loop bring the ribbon back to the center of the bow.*

4. *Twist in the center and add another loop. Twisting not only places the ribbon on the correct side, but it also gives the bow added body.*

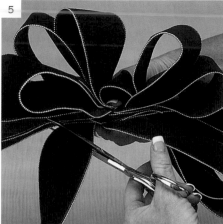

5. *Continue to twist the ribbon and repeat making loops continuously from side to side, each loop slightly larger until your bow is as full as desired. Continue to hold the bow pinched with your fingers around the center, and cut your ribbon from the bolt, close to the bow.*

6. *Continue holding the bow pinched with your fingers, and add your desired length of ribbon for the streamers.*

7. *Secure your bow by threading a floral wire through it. Pull the wire evenly through the bow.*

8. *Bring the wire ends to the back of the bow and twist tightly around the center of the bow. Adjust the loops attractively on both sides. Trim the ends of the streamers with a diagonal or V–cut.*

17

Introduction to the Projects

Now you are ready to begin creating dazzling arrangements for holidays throughout the year. Beginning with New Year's in January and continuing through to Christmas, you will create festive arrangements to add to the overal feel of the holidays. Simply follow the step-by-step instructions, and pay attention to the special tips and techniques. Feel free to add your own creative touches to the arrangements. You will want to proudly display these floral decorations throughout the year.

◆

New Year's Centerpiece

NEW YEAR'S IS A TIME FOR CELEBRATING THE PROMISE OF A NEW YEAR WITH FAMILY AND FRIENDS. WITH SILVER AND GOLD ACCENTS, THIS ARRANGEMENT MAKES A SPECTACULAR CENTERPIECE, PERFECT FOR A NEW YEAR'S PARTY. AT MIDNIGHT, LIGHT THE CENTERPIECE'S CANDLE, AND RING IN THE NEW YEAR WITH A CHAMPAGNE TOAST.

MATERIALS:

• 2 magnolia stems • 2 stems of gold hanging cockscomb • 3 10" (25cm) bubbled and glittered cedar sprays • 2 24" (61cm) clusters of silver branch stems • 1 30" (76cm) cluster of gold birch twigs • Spanish moss • 10" (25cm) tall ceramic urn • 2 10" (25cm) gold glittered star tree toppers • 12" (30cm) gold tapered candle • 2 yards (2m) gold and silver wired ribbon • gold spray paint • 2" (5cm) thick green floral sheet foam • greening pins • floral adhesive tape • green floral tape • floral pick extenders • glue gun • wire cutters

1: Lightly Spray the Moss Gold

Lay the Spanish moss out flat and lightly spray with gold spray paint.

2: Prepare the Container

Follow the instructions on pages 13–14 for preparing your container. Stack pieces of floral foam and attach them securely to the container with floral adhesive tape. The foam should extend 1" (3cm) above the top of the container. Cover the foam with the Spanish moss you sprayed gold, and secure it with greening pins.

3: Insert the Star Tree Toppers

Place one star in the center of the urn with the opening facing up. This will be used as the candle holder. Insert the other star off to the right side. Secure the stars in the foam with a glue gun.

4: Add the Magnolias

Cut one magnolia stem to 6" (15cm) and another to 4" (10cm). Save any leftover leaves for the next step. Place the taller magnolia in front of and slightly to the left of the middle star. Place the other magnolia off to the right of the center star and slightly lower than the first magnolia.

5

5: ADD THE REMAINING MAGNOLIA LEAVES

Attach the stems of the leaves to floral picks for added support, as shown on page 15. Insert the leaves around the magnolia flowers.

6

7

6: ADD CEDAR SPRAYS

Add one 10" (25cm) cedar spray to the left side of the arrangement, and place another 10" (25cm) spray on the right side, behind the right star.

7: SEPARATE AND ADD THE THIRD CEDAR SPRAY

Snip the third cedar spray into three sprigs, each with a 2" (5cm) stem. Place one sprig in the front between the magnolias. Place the other two in the back of the arrangement, behind the center star.

8: INSERT THE COCKSCOMB

Cut the gold cockscomb stems to 4" (10cm). Place one in the front left corner of the arrangement and the other in the back right, behind the center star.

8

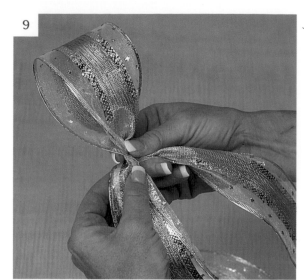

9

9: Make the Bows

For this project, you will need to make two bows. Cut the 2 yards (2m) of ribbon in half. Begin the first bow by pinching the ribbon between your fingers approximately 6" (15cm) from the end. This end piece will become the first streamer of the bow. Twist the ribbon with your fingers and form a small loop. Twist the ribbon in the center. Make another loop leaving an 8" (20cm) piece of ribbon for another streamer. Each bow has a total of two loops. For more detailed instruction on making bows, see pages 16–17.

10

11

10: Secure the Bows with Wire

To secure each bow, attach it to a floral pick extender by wrapping it with the wire. Wrap the excess wire down the floral pick.

11: Add the Bows to the Arrangement

Place one bow on the right side of the arrangement, between the star and the magnolia. Place the second bow to the left of the center star and toward the back of the arrangement.

12: Add the Silver Branches

Use branches that measure approximately 24" (61cm) long. Take one cluster and place it behind the center star. Snip the other cluster into three sections, then place one vertically in front of the center star, and the other two to the right and lower left of the center star.

12

13: ADD GOLD TWIGS
AND THE CANDLE

*Insert a cluster of gold birch twigs,
measuring approximately 30"
(76cm), slightly left of center, behind
the center star. Place one 12" (30cm)
tapered candle into the center star.*

DESIGNER idea

◆

Personalize

YOUR ARRANGEMENT BY ADDING

THE YEAR TO THE CENTER STAR

WITH RED OR BLUE GLITTER

GLUE. TO CREATE A VARIATION,

USE POINSETTIAS OR

LARGE LILIES IN PLACE OF THE

MAGNOLIAS.

Valentine's Day Arrangement

DELIGHT YOUR SWEETHEART WITH THIS ARRANGEMENT OF RED VELVET ROSES ON VALENTINE'S DAY. GIVE IT TO SOMEONE YOU LOVE OR DECORATE YOUR HOME TO CELEBRATE THIS VERY SPECIAL HOLIDAY. THE HEART-SHAPED GRAPEVINE WREATH GIVES THIS ARRANGEMENT SOME HEIGHT, WHICH MAKES THIS PIECE PERFECT FOR A SIDE TABLE IN A DINING ROOM OR ON A TABLE IN A FRONT ENTRYWAY.

MATERIALS:

• *12 red velvet roses* • *English ivy bush* • *Spanish moss* • *6" x 6" (15cm x 15cm) weathered stone container* • *14" (36cm) heart–shaped grapevine wreath*
• *4 yards (4m) festive wired ribbon* • *gold spray paint* • *gold glitter spray*
• *2" (5cm) thick green floral sheet foam* • *greening pins* • *floral pick extenders*
• *floral adhesive tape* • *green floral tape* • *22–gauge floral wire* • *heavy wire or extra flower stems* • *glue gun* • *wire cutters*

1: PREPARE THE CONTAINER

Stack three pieces of floral foam and attach them securely to the container with floral adhesive tape and greening pins. Refer to the basic technique, Preparing Your Container With Foam, on pages 13–14. Cover the foam with Spanish moss and secure it with greening pins.

2: CREATE GOLD ACCENTS

Lightly spray the heart wreath with gold spray paint to create gold accents.

3: ADD RIBBON TO THE WREATH

Lay the ribbon on the wreath, following the heart shape. Secure the ribbon to the wreath using a glue gun. Repeat this step on the other side of the wreath if you want it to be finished on both sides.

4: ADD THE HEART WREATH TO THE CONTAINER

Cut two 8" (20cm) pieces of heavy flower stems, or a heavy wire such as a clothes hanger. Bend each in half to form a loop. Place the heart in the center of the container. Secure the wreath with the two wire loops, one in front of the grapevine and one in back. If the heart seems wobbly, take the wires out and cover them with hot glue, then press in securely.

5: Add Ivy to the Wreath

Using wire cutters, separate the ivy trailers from the ivy bush. Cut four 24"
(61cm) ivy trailers. Starting at the top, wrap an ivy trailer around the heart
and secure it by twisting the wired end into the wreath. Do the same thing with
each trailer. When you finish, ivy should look like it is naturally growing
throughout the wreath.

 tip

IF YOU WOULD LIKE THE GRAPEVINE WREATH TO HAVE A

FULLER LOOK, ADD MORE IVY TRAILERS.

6: Add Greenery to the Container

Cut ten 12" (30cm) sprigs of ivy. Add floral pick extenders to the ends of the
ivy, and place the sprigs randomly around the pot. Don't be too concerned
about the placement; it should look whimsical, like it is growing naturally.

7: Add the Velvet Roses

Cut the twelve roses to 8" (20cm). Place six of the roses around the center
and six going outward from the wreath.

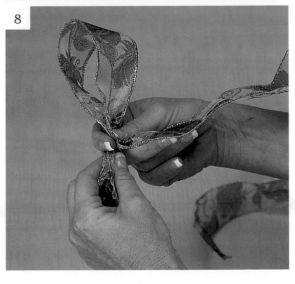

8: Start the Bow

To create the bow, cut 2 yards (2m) of ribbon. Leave 6" (15cm) for a streamer
and make a loop using 9" (23cm). Twist the ribbon in the center.

9: FINISH THE BOW

Make a total of five 9" (23cm) loops. Remember to twist in the center before making the next loop. Secure the bow in the center with a piece of floral wire.

10: ADD THE BOW TO THE WREATH

Place the bow in the center of the heart and fasten it with the wire used to make the bow. Trim and hide the wires within the grapevine.

11: ADD TWO SMALLER BOWS

Using 1 yard (1m) of ribbon for each bow, create two more bows. These two bows will have only two loops per bow with 6" (15cm) streamers. Secure the bows in the center with a floral pick extender. Insert one bow at the front right side and one at the left, on the back side of the heart wreath.

12: ADD FINAL TOUCHES

Spray the entire arrangement with glitter spray. Shape the flowers and the ivy and give it a natural look.

DESIGNER **idea**

✦

Add a romantic

TOUCH TO THIS ARRANGEMENT,

BY PLACING A PORCELAIN CUPID

OR OTHER COLLECTIBLE

FIGURINE IN THE CENTER OF IT

FOR ADDED INTEREST.

Blooming Easter Wreath

THIS GRAPEVINE WREATH WILL BE A WELCOME SIGHT

ON YOUR PORCH OR FRONT DOOR. WHILE THE EASTER EGGS ARE UNIQUE TO THE

HOLIDAY, THE BLOOMING HYACINTHS, CROCUSES, PANSIES AND TULIPS ADD THE

BEAUTIFUL COLORS WE SO LOOK FORWARD TO IN THE SPRING.

MATERIALS:

- 1 hyacinth bush with 6 stems • 1 10" (25cm) crocus bush with 6 stems
- 3 mini tulip stems • 4 pansy stems with 5 blooms per stem • 3 freesia stems
with 2 blooms per stem • 1 amaranthus stem with 5 trailers • 3 variegated ivy
trailers • dried Malian grass or silk grass • 20" (51cm) moss—covered
grapevine wreath • 5 wooden Easter eggs • 5 yards (5m) festive sheer wired
ribbon • floral pick extenders • green floral tape • 22—gauge floral wire
• glue gun • wire cutters • drill

1: ADD HYACINTHS TO THE WREATH

Take a hyacinth bush with six flowers and snip off the two blooms on the outside. Place the stem with four blooms in the center of the wreath. Insert the remaining two blooms to the lower left and right of the center hyacinths. Secure the hyacinths to the wreath with a glue gun.

2: ADD THE CROCUS BUSH

Place the crocus bush with six blooms just below the hyacinth bush and secure with a glue gun.

3: INSERT THE TULIPS

Cut the three tulips to 9" (23cm) and place them within and around the crocus bush. Secure again with glue.

4: ADD PANSIES

Snip off each individual pansy stem from the bush. Insert one stem higher in the arrangement within the hyacinths. Insert one at the lower left, facing out of the wreath. Insert one at the lower right facing the inner circle of the wreath. Insert one facing downward from the wreath in the right corner. Secure with a glue gun.

5: ADD THE FREESIA

Cut one stem of freesia to 20" (51cm) and two to 13" (33cm). Place the longest stem above and within the hyacinths, so it is extending above them. Place the other stems at the lower left and right of the arrangement. If necessary, use a glue gun.

6: ADD THE AMARANTHUS

Insert the amaranthus below the arrangement. It should hang down from the wreath.

7: ADD GREENERY

Cut two ivy trailers to 18" (46cm) and one to 14" (36cm). Place the shorter trailer down toward the bottom left of the arrangement. Place one of the longer ones in the center facing downward within the amaranthus, and insert the other to the right of the center trailer also facing downward. They all should hang down from the wreath. Secure with a glue gun.

8: MAKE A BOW

Create a bow with a total of eight loops and four streamers. First, cut off 1 yard (1m) from the 4 yards (4m) of ribbon. This will become two of the streamers. With the remaining ribbon, leave 18" (46cm) for a streamer, and then make a loop using 13" (33cm) of ribbon. Twist the ribbon in the center. Make a total of eight loops using approximately 13" (33cm) of ribbon in each loop. Remember to twist each loop in the center before creating the next loop. Add the two remaining streamers by folding the 1 yard (1m) of ribbon in half. Secure the bow in the center with floral wire.

9: Add the Bow to the Wreath

Add the bow to the wreath under the arrangement of flowers and above the trailing greenery and amaranthus. Use the floral wire in the center of the bow to fasten the bow to the wreath.

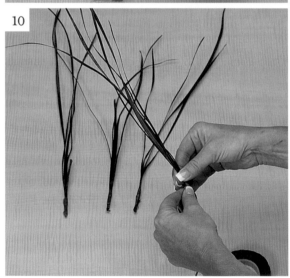

10: Make Grass Clusters

Make four bundles of grass using five or six pieces of grass per bundle. Using green floral tape, bind each bundle together.

11: Add Grass to the Wreath

Insert the four bundles of grass throughout the arrangement of flowers on the wreath. Secure them with a glue gun.

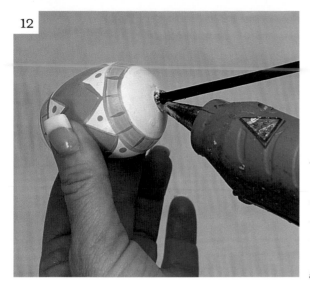

12: PREPARE AND ADD THE WOODEN EGGS

Using a ¼" (7mm) bit, drill a small hole in the bottom of each egg. Cut the wires off five floral pick extenders. Using a glue gun, secure a floral pick inside the hole of each egg. Insert the eggs randomly throughout the arrangement. Place three around the bow and two off to the right side of the wreath. Hold in place with glue from a glue gun.

DESIGNER idea

◆

Welcome IN THE

SPRING SEASON BY REMOVING

THE EGGS AFTER EASTER.

Easter Vase *Arrangement*

THIS EASTER ARRANGEMENT WILL LOOK AS THOUGH YOU BROUGHT FRESH BLOSSOMS FROM OUTSIDE TO BRIGHTEN YOUR HOME INSIDE. EARLY SPRING FLOWERS WITH ASSORTED GRASSES, CREATE THE PERFECT PIECE TO CELEBRATE THE EASTER HOLIDAY.

MATERIALS:

• *3 delphinium stems* • *4 daffodil blooms open* • *3 daffodil buds* • *4 hyacinths*
• *4 10" (25cm) iris stems* • *4 primula stems* • *dried Malian grass* • *green curly willow branches* • *3 14" (36cm) silk Easter grass stems* • *4 English ivy stems* • *3 senecio vines* • *8 wooden Easter eggs* • *4 yards (4m) festive sheer wired ribbon* • *Spanish moss* • *10" (25cm) tall green ceramic container* • *2" (5cm) thick green floral sheet foam* • *greening pins* • *floral pick extenders* • *floral adhesive tape* • *green floral tape* • *glue gun* • *wire cutters* • *drill*

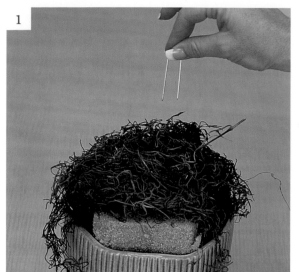

1: PREPARE THE CONTAINER

Stack pieces of foam to the top of the vase and attach them securely to the container with floral adhesive tape and greening pins. Cover the foam with moss and secure with greening pins.

2: ADD DAFFODIL BLOOMS

Cut the daffodil blooms, one to 20" (51cm) and three to 18" (46cm). Place the tallest in the center of the foam and the remaining three just beneath and around the center daffodil.

3: ADD THE DAFFODIL BUDS

Cut the three daffodil buds to 17" (43cm), and intersperse them between the daffodils.

4: ADD THE DELPHINIUM AND HYACINTHS

Cut the three delphinium stems to 20" (51cm) and insert them in the center within the daffodils. Cut one hyacinth to 14" (36cm) and three to 12" (30cm). Place the tallest hyacinth in the center of the arrangement. Place the other three proportionally around the arrangement below the daffodils.

5: ADD THE IRIS STEMS AND ENGLISH IVY

Cut the four iris stems to 6" (15cm) and place them proportionally around the arrangement. Add the greenery from the iris stems behind the iris blooms. Next, place a stem of English ivy, cut to 8" (20cm), below each iris.

6: ADD THE SENECIO VINE

Place the three 14" (36cm) senecio vines proportionally around the bottom of the arrangement.

7: ADD THE EASTER GRASS

Insert the three stems of Easter grass proportionally around the center within the daffodils.

special note: *If you cannot locate Easter grass, use another type of grass or more of the Malian grass used in step 10.*

8: PREPARE WILLOW BRANCHES

Cut six pieces of curly willow branches to 18"–20" (46cm–51cm). Bind the branches together using green floral tape. Make a total of three bundles.

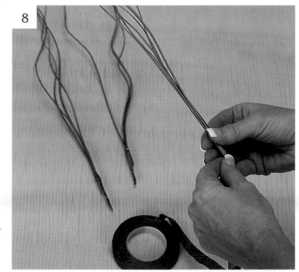

9: Add the Willow Branches

Place the three willow branch bundles in the center of the arrangement.

10: Add the Malian Grass

Cut six pieces of Malian grass to 10"–12" (25cm–30cm). Bind the pieces together with green floral tape. Make a total of three bundles. Insert the Malian grass in and around the hyacinths.

11: Add the Primula

Cut the primula stems to 10" (25cm). Arrange the four clustered stems around the bottom of the arrangement.

12: Make the Bows

For this project, you will need two bows. Each bow requires approximately 2 yards (2m) of ribbon. Start the first bow by leaving an 8" (20cm) streamer and making a loop using approximately 10" (25cm) of ribbon. Twist the ribbon. Make another 10" (25cm) loop and twist again. Repeat this step until you have four loops of the same size. Cut the ribbon, leaving another 8" (20cm) streamer. Secure the bow in the center with a floral pick extender. Repeat these steps for the second bow.

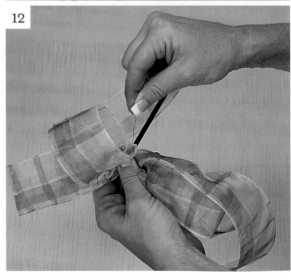

13

14

*Use a ¼" (7mm) drill bit to make a
small hole in the bottom of each egg.
Cut the wires off of the floral pick
extenders. Using a glue gun, glue a
floral pick inside the hole of each
egg. Place the eggs randomly around
the bottom of the arrangement.*

13: Add the Bows to the Arrangement

Place the two bows on either side of the arrangement, between the irises.

DESIGNER idea

✦

This arrangement

BEAUTIFULLY COMPLEMENTS

THE EASTER WREATH. DISPLAY

BOTH PROJECTS IN YOUR HOME

FOR THE EASTER HOLIDAY.

Mother's Day Arrangement

THIS ARRANGEMENT IS FULL OF SOFTLY COLORED FLOWERS. THE ROSES AND LILIES SYMBOLIZE A SPECIAL KIND OF LOVE, WHILE THE SOFT COLORS REPRESENT A MOTHER'S GENTLENESS. THESE ARE QUALITIES THAT REMIND ME OF MY MOTHER. WHEN YOU MAKE THIS ARRANGEMENT, THINK OF HOW YOU WOULD DESCRIBE YOUR OWN MOTHER, AND FILL IT WITH FLOWERS THAT REMIND YOU OF HER.

MATERIALS:

• 3 white rose stems • 2 lily stems with buds • 2 globe thistle stems • 1 violet bush • 1 55" (1.4m) wispy green willow branch • English ivy bush • Spanish moss • 7"x7"x6" (18cm x 18cm x 15cm) square carton container • 2⅓ yards (2.1m) sheer wired ribbon • 2" (5cm) thick green floral sheet foam • greening pins • floral pick extenders • floral adhesive tape • green floral tape • 22—gauge floral wire • wire cutters

1: PREPARE THE CONTAINER

Stack three pieces of floral foam and attach them securely to the container with floral adhesive tape and greening pins. Cover the foam with Spanish moss, and secure it with greening pins.

2: ADD THE LILIES

Cut lily stems to 13" (33cm). Place one lily stem diagonally upward at the right and one diagonally down at the front left side of the container.

3: ADD the ROSES AND VIOLET BUSH

Cut the rose stem to 20" (51cm) and insert it in the back left, between the lilies. Insert a small violet bush in the front right corner of the container.

4: ADD THE GLOBE THISTLE

*Cut one globe thistle stem to 20"
(51cm), and another to 15" (38cm).
Place the longer one left of center, next
to the rose stem. Insert the shorter stem
behind the lower-left lily stem.*

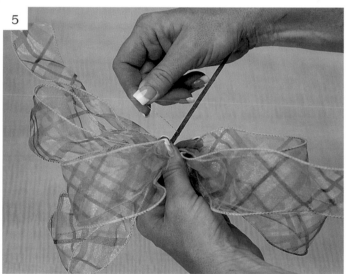

5: CREATE THE BOW

*To make this bow, leave a 9" (23cm) streamer and then make a loop, using
10" (25cm) of ribbon. Twist the ribbon in the center. Make a total of six
loops, each time twisting the ribbon before creating the next loop. Secure the
bow in the center with the wire from a floral pick extender. Wrap the excess
wire down the floral pick.*

6: ADD THE BOW TO THE ARRANGEMENT

Place the bow in the center of the arrangement, between the violets and the lilies.

7: SNIP AND INSERT THE WILLOW BRANCH

Cut the willow branch into two separate branches, making one approximately 28" (71cm) and one 19" (48cm). Insert the longer willow branch left of center and behind the globe thistle stem. Insert the other willow branch within the lower-left globe thistle stem and lilies.

8

8: ADD ENGLISH IVY TRAILERS

Cut two ivy trailers to 15" (38cm). Place them on either side of the lilies. Cut four or five ivy stems to 6"– 8" (15cm–20cm), and place throughout the arrangement, filling in any holes.

DESIGNER **idea**

✦

Create a

ONE-OF-A-KIND GIFT FOR

MOTHER'S DAY BY SELECTING

HER FAVORITE FLOWERS AND

COLORS. WITH SILK FLOWERS,

SHE'LL BE ABLE TO ENJOY IT

ALL YEAR ROUND.

Father's Day Arrangement

INSTEAD OF THE USUAL NECKTIE OR GOLF BALLS, GIVE DAD A UNIQUE ARRANGEMENT FOR FATHER'S DAY. THIS PIECE WOULD LOOK GREAT ON A MANTEL IN A LIVING ROOM, IN AN OFFICE ON A CREDENZA OR FILE CABINET OR IN A DEN ON A BOOKSHELF. SHOW HIM HOW MUCH HE MEANS TO YOU WITH THIS ARRANGEMENT MADE ESPECIALLY FOR HIM.

MATERIALS:

• 2 10" (25cm) water lily stems with bulb and 3 leaves • 1 17" (43cm) anthurium stem • 4 cattail stems • 4 8" (20cm) tea leaf stems • 2 15" (38cm) mini needle ivy stems with 5 trailers per stem • 1 12" (30cm) grass bundle • birch branches • Spanish moss • 11" x 10" x 6" (28cm x 25cm x 15cm) trunk with lid • 12" x 5" (30cm x 13cm) wooden duck • 2" (5cm) thick green floral sheet foam • greening pins • floral pick extenders • floral adhesive tape • green floral tape • wire cutters

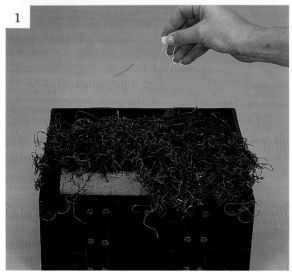

1: PREPARE THE CONTAINER

To cut and secure the foam in the trunk, refer to the basic technique, Preparing Your Container With Foam on pages 13–14. Cover the foam with Spanish moss, and secure it with greening pins.

2: ADD THE WOODEN DUCK

Place a strip of floral adhesive on the bottom of the duck. Clear the moss from the center of the trunk and press the duck firmly on the foam.

3: Add the Water Lilies and Anthurium

Place one 10" (25cm) lily at the right back, behind the head of the duck. Place the other 10" (25cm) lily at the left front of the trunk. Twist this lily and the leaves down closer to the bulb and sprouts. Cut the anthurium to 17" (43cm) and place it behind the lily and the duck.

4: Add Cattails

Cut one cattail to 30" (76cm), one to 24" (61cm), one to 12" (30cm) and one to 8" (20cm). Place the two tallest cattails behind the back lily. Insert the 12" (30cm) cattail angled to the right front of the trunk, and the shortest cattail in the front left side of the trunk, behind the water lily.

5: Add the Mini Needle Ivy

Insert one 15" (38cm) mini needle ivy stem into the lower—right side of the trunk and the other 15" (38cm) stem into the lower—left side of the trunk.

6: INSERT THE TEA LEAVES

The tea leaves make a subtle difference in the foliage of this arrangement, really pulling the piece together. Place three 8" (20cm) stems of tea leaves in the lower front, side and back of the right side of the arrangement. Place the fourth 8" (20cm) stem into the lower—left side of the trunk.

7: PREPARE THE GRASS

Snip off eight to ten blades of grass and bind to a floral pick with green floral tape. Repeat this step, making three 12" (30cm) bundles of grass. The remainder of the grass left on the store—bought bundle will be used as a fourth and larger bundle.

8: INSERT THE GRASS BUNDLES

Place the remainder of the 12" (30cm) store—bought bundle behind the tallest cattails. This gives the arrangement height and dimension. Place the remaining three bundles just outside and around the center of the arrangement.

9

9: ADD BIRCH TWIGS

Insert a cluster of 22" (56cm) birch twigs in the center of the arrangement next to the tallest cattails. Place a cluster of 15" (38cm) birch twigs at the lower—left and right sides of the trunk. Place a 12" (30cm) cluster of twigs, angled upward, at the right side of the trunk.

DESIGNER **idea**

✦

Personalize

THIS ARRANGEMENT BY

REPLACING THE WOODEN

DUCK WITH A FIGURINE, PLAQUE

OR OTHER COLLECTIBLE TO

SUIT THE INTEREST OF

YOUR FATHER.

Fourth of July Basket

FOR THAT FOURTH OF JULY BARBECUE OR PARTY, THIS

BEAUTIFUL PICNIC BASKET IS A FESTIVE ADDITION TO A SUNROOM OR PATIO. IT IS

ALSO A WONDERFUL ARRANGEMENT TO DISPLAY ALL SEASON, FROM MEMORIAL DAY

TO LABOR DAY. PROUDLY DISPLAY YOUR PATRIOTISM AND CELEBRATE SUMMERTIME!

MATERIALS:

• 2 18" (46cm) geranium bushes with 5 full blooms and 3 buds • 1 daisy bush
with 8 blooms • dusty miller bush • 1 16" (41cm) variegated ivy bush with
trailers • 18" x 12" x 8" (46cm x 30cm x 20cm) picnic basket • 4 ½ yards
(4.5m) patriotic ribbon • 2" (5cm) thick green floral sheet foam • floral pick
extenders • floral adhesive tape • green floral tape • 22–gauge floral wire
• glue gun • wire cutters

1: Prepare the Basket

Cut an 18" (46cm) piece of floral foam and attach securely to the basket with strips of floral adhesive. Use only one layer of foam so the flowers will be tucked inside and appear to grow out of the basket.

2: Add the Geranium Bushes

With the lids of the basket propped open, insert a geranium bush in the center of both of the openings of the basket.

3: Add Daisies

Daisy stems usually come in bush form, so snip the stems 15" (38cm) long, add floral pick extenders and insert them into the foam. You need four daisy stems with each geranium bush. Place the daisies just beneath and around the geraniums.

4: ADD THE DUSTY MILLER BUSH

Cut the dusty miller bush into four individual stems measuring 12" (30cm). Intersperse the dusty miller with the foliage from the geranium bushes. Attach a floral pick extender if you need added length.

5: ADD THE VARIEGATED IVY

Cut the variegated ivy bush apart and insert three 16" (41cm) trailers around the bottom of the arrangement. Insert the trailers up next to the geranium bush, near the handle. The trailers should hang over the edge of the basket so the ivy appears to be growing downward.

6: ADD RIBBON TO THE BASKET

Measure enough ribbon to fit around the outside of the basket, and secure it with a glue gun.

7: BEGIN THE BOW

For this bow you will need 2½ yards (2.5m) of patriotic ribbon. Start by cutting 20" (51cm) for the streamers. Then, pinch the remaining ribbon to make a small center loop. This will become the "knot" of the bow.

8: FINISH THE BOW

Twist the ribbon in the center, and make a loop using approximately 10" (25cm) of ribbon. Do this for the first two loops and then gradually make the loops larger by using about 12"–14" (30cm – 36cm) for each loop. Make a total of six loops and remember to twist the ribbon after each loop you make. Use the 20" (51cm) you cut off in step 7 for the streamers, and secure the bow with floral wire.

9: ATTACH THE BOW

Add the bow to the basket by weaving the floral wire you used to secure the bow through the basket. Twist the wires together on the inside of the basket. Adjust the bow once it is attached to give it a full shape.

DESIGNER **idea**

✦

This versatile

BASKET CAN BE USED YEAR ROUND.
TO CELEBRATE BIRTHDAYS,
FAVORITE SPORTS TEAMS OR OTHER
SUMMER OCCASIONS, SIMPLY
CHANGE THE RIBBON. USE
DAFFODILS AND TULIPS IN THE
SPRING, MUMS IN THE FALL AND
POINSETTIAS IN THE WINTER.

Halloween Jack O' Lantern

ENTERTAIN THOSE TRICK-OR-TREATERS WHO COME TO YOUR DOOR WITH THIS HALLOWEEN ARRANGEMENT. THE MUMS AND LEAVES WILL LOOK LIKE YOU JUST PICKED THEM FROM OUTSIDE. WHETHER YOUR HALLOWEEN PLANS INCLUDE COSTUME PARTIES, HAYRIDES OR BOBBING FOR APPLES, ENJOY THE HOLIDAY WITH THIS ARRANGEMENT.

MATERIALS:

- *2 gold mum stems with 3 blooms per stem* • *2 burgundy mum stems with 2 blooms per stem* • *2 eucalyptus stems with 5 sprigs per stem* • *6 eucalyptus stems with berries* • *7 6" (15cm) wired fall leaves* • *2 bare branch twigs*
- *Spanish moss* • *9" (23cm) diameter copper container, 4" (10cm) deep*
- *11" tall (28cm) foam jack o' lantern* • *2" (5cm) thick green floral sheet foam*
- *greening pins* • *floral pick extenders* • *floral adhesive tape* • *green floral tape*
- *wire cutters*

1: PREPARE THE CONTAINER

Stack three pieces of floral foam and attach them to the container with floral adhesive tape and greening pins. Cover the foam with Spanish moss, securing it with greening pins.

2: ADD THE PUMPKIN

Place the pumpkin on top of the foam, moving moss so it can sit securely. You can place floral adhesive on the bottom of the pumpkin if it seems wobbly.

3: ADD THE AUTUMN LEAVES

Cut off seven leaves and add floral pick extenders if necessary. The overall length of each leaf with a floral pick extender should be 8" (20cm). Insert the leaves proportionally around the pumpkin and close to the container.

4: Prepare the Gold Mums

This particular mum stem came in a cluster of three with one bud, one small bloom and one large bloom. Cut the two buds to 12" (30cm), the two small blooms to 10" (25cm) and the two large blooms to 5" (13cm).

5: Insert the Gold Mums

Insert the 12" (30cm) buds to the right and left sides of the pumpkin. Insert the two smaller blooms in front of the buds. Place the large blooms on either side of the pumpkin.

6: Add the Burgundy Mums

Cut the stem of a large mum to 4" (10cm), and insert it toward the front right side of the pumpkin. Add another mum toward the back left side of the container. Cut the stems of two smaller burgundy mums to 7" (18cm), and insert one angled to the front left and one toward the back right sides of the container.

tip

FOR A WONDERFUL AROMA, USE FRESH
EUCALYPTUS. IT WILL DRY NATURALLY
IN THE ARRANGEMENT AND LAST THROUGH-
OUT THE SEASON.

7: ADD THE EUCALYPTUS WITH BERRIES

Cut the six stems of eucalyptus with berries to 10" (25cm). Insert one stem between each mum, circling the arrangement.

8: SEPARATE THE EUCALYPTUS SPRIGS

Take two stems of eucalyptus with five sprigs per stem and cut the two end sprigs off, leaving the three in the center clustered together.

9: ADD MORE EUCALYPTUS

Place the two eucalyptus stems with three pieces clustered together within the gold mums on either side of the pumpkin.

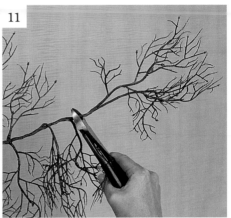

11: Separate and Add the Bare Twigs

Cut the bare twig branches into twelve small twig clusters, approximately 10" (25cm) long. Insert them randomly throughout the arrangement.

10: Add the Remaining Eucalyptus

Insert the remaining eucalyptus sprigs randomly around the arrangement, filling in where needed.

DESIGNER idea

♦

With silk flowers

AND FOLIAGE, THIS
ARRANGEMENT WILL LAST FOR
MANY HALLOWEEN SEASONS.
USE A CARVED FOAM PUMPKIN
TO CELEBRATE HALLOWEEN,
AND THEN REPLACE THE
JACK O' LANTERN WITH A
REGULAR PUMPKIN FOR THE
REMAINDER OF AUTUMN.

Thanksgiving
Autumn Basket

THIS FALL BASKET ARRANGEMENT IS SURE TO BRIGHTEN ANY ROOM DURING THE AUTUMN SEASON. I COMBINED THE FLOWERS AS IF THEY WERE A GROWING POTTED PLANT, GIVING THE ARRANGEMENT A NATURAL LOOK THAT WOULD ENHANCE YOUR FRONT PORCH OR FIREPLACE HEARTH. THIS PIECE ALSO MAKES AN INVITING CENTERPIECE ON A DINING ROOM TABLE. CELEBRATE THANKSGIVING WITH THIS SIMPLE ARRANGEMENT TO REMIND YOU OF ALL LIFE'S SIMPLE PLEASURES.

MATERIALS:

• 6 18" (46cm) black–eyed susan stems with 4 blooms per stem • 6 14" (30cm) marigold stems with 3 blooms per stem • 5 charm marigold stems with 7 blooms per stem • 1 viburnum bush • 2 burbrush stems • 1 variegated ivy bush • Spanish moss • 10" x 16" x 7" (25cm x 41cm x 18cm) oval basket • 2" (5cm) thick green floral sheet foam • greening pins • floral pick extenders • floral adhesive tape • green floral tape • wire cutters

1: Prepare the Container

To cut and secure the foam in your basket, refer to the basic technique, Preparing Your Container With Foam, on pages 13–14. Cover the foam with Spanish moss, and secure it with greening pins.

2: Add Black–eyed Susans & Marigolds

Cut the black-eyed susan stems to 18" (46cm), and center them in a cluster at the right side of the basket. Cut the marigold stems to 14" (36cm) and place them around the left side of the basket.

3: Add the Charm Marigolds

Place the charm marigolds under the black–eyed susans, on the right side of the basket.

4: Insert the Viburnum into the Basket

Separate the stems of viburnum from the bush and place six stems around the arrangement, within the marigolds.

5

6

6: Add the Ivy Trailers

Separate the ivy trailers, ranging from 14"–22" (36cm–56cm) long, from the bush. Add floral pick extenders to the stems to give added strength. Insert the stems around the outer edges of the arrangement to fill in where needed. The trailers should hang over the edge of the basket.

5: Add the Burbrush Stems

Place the two 26" (66cm) burbrush stems in the center of the basket, within the black-eyed susans.

tip

If you cannot locate burbrush stems, you may substitute cattails.

designer idea

◆

The beauty OF THIS ARRANGEMENT IS IN ITS VERSATILITY. FOR INSTANCE, YOU MAY WANT TO USE SUNFLOWERS IN PLACE OF BLACK-EYED SUSANS. PERSONALIZE THIS PIECE WITH YOUR FAVORITE FALL FLOWERS.

Thanksgiving Harvest Arrangement

WELCOME FAMILY AND FRIENDS TO YOUR HOME FOR THANKSGIVING DINNER WITH THIS BEAUTIFUL ARRANGEMENT. THE CONTAINER IS FLAT ON ONE SIDE AND WOULD BE GORGEOUS ON A FRONT DOOR OR HANGING INSIDE ON A WALL. THE GOURDS AND WHEAT REALLY CELEBRATE THE AUTUMN HARVEST WITH THE BEAUTY OF RICH FALL COLORS.

73

MATERIALS:

• 4 large sunflowers • 3 large mums • 4 bittersweet branches • 3 mini fall leaf trailers • 1 ivy bush • 1 wheat bundle • 5 red fall leaf stems • 3 small foam pumpkins and/or gourds • Spanish moss • 18" x 10" (46cm x 25cm) flat-backed copper container • 2½ yards (2.5m) festive wired ribbon • 2" (5cm) thick green floral sheet foam • greening pins • floral pick extenders • floral adhesive tape • green floral tape • glue gun • wire cutters • paring knife

1: Prepare the Container

Refer to the basic technique, Preparing Your Container with Foam, on pages 13–14 to fit foam into this container. Stack two pieces of foam together so they fit snugly, and leave about 1" (3cm) of foam sticking out of the container. Cover the foam with Spanish moss and secure it with greening pins.

2: Add the Sunflowers

Cut one sunflower stem to 22" (56cm), one to 14" (36cm), one to 10" (25cm) and one to 6" (15cm). Insert the tallest stem in the middle of the container. Insert the 14" (36cm) stem left of the center and toward the back. Insert the 10" (25cm) stem in the center of the container and in front of the tallest stem. Finally, insert the 6" (15cm) stem to the left of the arrangement at the front of the container.

3: Add the Mums

Cut one mum stem to 12" (30cm), one to 9" (23cm), and one to 6" (15cm). Insert them diagonally to the left, starting with the tallest in the upper-right corner, and ending with the shortest stem in the lower-left corner. The shortest stem should be inserted at a downward angle so that it is hanging over the edge of the container.

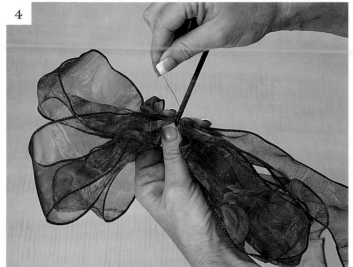

4: CREATE THE BOW

Leaving a 20" (51cm) streamer, make a loop using 12" (30cm) of ribbon, then twist the ribbon. Make another loop the same size as the first loop, then twist. Repeat this step until you have five loops of the same size. Cut the ribbon leaving another 20" (51cm) streamer. Secure the bow in the center with a floral pick extender.

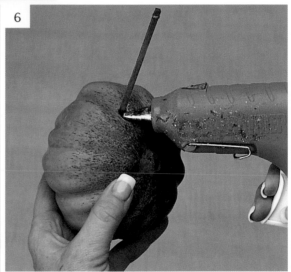

6: PREPARE THE PUMPKINS AND GOURDS

Poke a small hole in each foam pumpkin and gourd with a paring knife. Cut the wires off the floral pick extenders. Secure the picks inside the holes of each pumpkin and gourd with a glue gun.

5: ADD THE BOW TO THE ARRANGEMENT

Insert the bow into the arrangement, left of center, under the sunflower.

7: Add the Pumpkins and Gourds to the Arrangement

Insert the two pumpkins to the right of the bow, along the rim of the container. Insert the gourd in the center, above the pumpkins.

8: Insert the Wheat Bundle into the Arrangement

Wrap a piece of 22–gauge wire around the bundle of wheat. Attach a floral pick extender to the wire. Insert the wheat in the center of the arrangement, placing it between the pumpkins and below the center sunflower.

9: Add Red Fall Leaves

Snip the stem of red fall leaves in 6" (15cm) sprigs and insert them throughout the arrangement, filling in where needed.

10: Add the Ivy Trailers

Snip off four ivy trailers from the ivy bush. Insert two 12" (30cm) trailers in the lower–left corner, trailing down with the ribbon. Insert one 14" (36cm) ivy trailer in the upper–right corner behind the tallest mum. Finally, insert another 12" (30cm) ivy trailer in the lower–right corner of the arrangement.

11

12

12: ADD THE
BITTERSWEET

*Cut one stem of bitter-
sweet to 24" (61cm),
one to 17" (45cm) and
two to 15" (38cm).
Insert the tallest stem
behind the tallest sun-
flower. Insert the 17"
(43cm) bittersweet in
the upper—left corner.
Insert the two shorter
stems at the left and right
sides of the arrangement.*

11: ADD MINI FALL LEAF TRAILERS

*Cut one stem to 24" (61cm), one to 18" (46cm) and two to 12"
(30cm). Insert the longest stem toward the bottom of the container,
within the ribbon streamers and ivy trailers. Insert the 18" (46cm)
stem to the right of the longest stem also within the ribbon. Insert the
two shorter stems on either side of the two longer stems. Bend the leaf
stems downward with the ivy and ribbon to create a flowing look.*

DESIGNER **idea**

✦

For added

NATURAL BEAUTY, USE REAL

MINI PUMPKINS AND GOURDS.

THEY WILL LAST FOR MONTHS,

THROUGH THE HOLIDAY

SEASON. BEFORE STORING,

REMOVE THE MINI PUMPKINS

AND GOURDS, SO THEY WILL

NOT MOLD AND RUIN THE

ARRANGEMENT.

Thanksgiving Cornucopia

CELEBRATE A TRADITIONAL THANKSGIVING WITH THIS CORNUCOPIA ARRANGEMENT. THE FALL LEAVES, GOURDS AND MUMS BRING OUT THE VERY BEST OF AUTUMN AND REMIND ME OF MY FAVORITE THANKSGIVING MEMORIES. THE UNIQUE WIRE CORNUCOPIA BECOMES THE BASE FOR A CANDLE, SO THIS ARRANGEMENT MAKES A LOVELY TABLE CENTERPIECE.

MATERIALS:

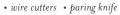

• *8 mum stems* • *6" (15cm) wired fall leaves* • *4 red fall leaf stems* • *1 wheat bundle with 8 stems* • *3 eucalyptus stems* • *6 mini foam gourds* • *Spanish moss* • *20" x 10" (51cm x 25cm) wire cornucopia* • *12" (30cm) tapered candle* • *Plastic taper candle holder* • *2" (5cm) thick green floral sheet foam* • *floral pick extenders* • *greening pins* • *green floral tape* • *22—gauge wire* • *glue gun* • *wire cutters* • *paring knife*

1: PREPARE THE FLORAL FOAM

Cut a piece of floral foam to fit snugly into the wired cornucopia. Cover the foam with Spanish moss and secure it with greening pins.

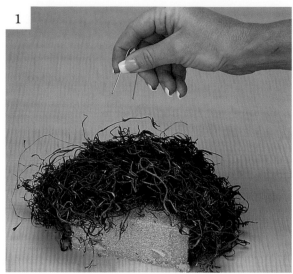

2: ADD THE FOAM AND CANDLE HOLDER TO THE CONTAINER

Secure the foam to the container by inserting a piece of floral wire through the wire basket and around the foam, twisting the ends together. Firmly insert the plastic taper candle holder in the center of the foam.

3: ADD LEAVES TO THE INSIDE OF THE CORNUCOPIA

Because this container is made of wire, the moss and foam are visible. In order to hide them, cover the moss with red fall leaves.

4: ADD THE WIRED AUTUMN LEAVES

Insert a wired leaf at the top, bottom and on each side of the cornucopia.

5: ADD THE EUCALYPTUS

Cut two stems of eucalyptus to 18" (46cm). Insert one in the upper—left corner and one in the bottom—right corner of the arrangement.

6: INSERT THE MUMS

Cut two mum stems to 12" (30cm) and insert them in front of the eucalyptus. Cut two mum stems to 9" (23cm), then insert one in the upper—right and one in the lower—left of the arrangement. Cut two mum stems to 7" (18cm) and insert them in front of the two longest mums, in the upper—left and lower—right corners. Cut the final two mum stems to 6" (15cm) and insert them in the center around the candle holder.

7: PREPARE AND INSERT THE GOURDS

Poke a small hole in each foam gourd with a paring knife. Cut the wire off a floral pick. Using a glue gun, glue a floral pick inside the hole of each gourd. Insert gourds randomly throughout the arrangement.

8: SEPARATE AND ADD MORE EUCALYPTUS

Snip the remaining eucalyptus stem into sprigs, ranging in size from 6"–10" (15cm–25cm) each. Insert the sprigs randomly throughout the arrangement, filling in where needed.

9: ADD THE WHEAT
BUNDLES AND THE CANDLE

Take eight stems of wheat and stagger them to different lengths. Bind the wheat together with a floral pick extender. Insert the wheat in the center of the arrangement, next to the candle holder. Finally, insert a 12" (30cm) tapered candle in the center of the arrangement.

DESIGNER **idea**

✦

Celebrate autumn

WITH REAL FALL LEAVES,
GOURDS AND PUMPKINS IN
THIS ARRANGEMENT. THEY
WILL LAST AS LONG AS THE
FALL SEASON. WHEN YOU
STORE THE ARRANGEMENT,
HOWEVER, REMEMBER TO
REMOVE THE REAL ITEMS,
BECAUSE THEY WILL
EVENTUALLY MOLD.

Christmas Topiary

THIS EXQUISITE TOPIARY MAKES A SOPHISTICATED

ADDITION TO YOUR CHRISTMAS DÉCOR. DISPLAY IT IN AN ENTRYWAY OR FORMAL

DINING ROOM DURING THE CHRISTMAS SEASON. THE PURPLE MAGNOLIAS AND GOLD

RIBBONS ARE REFRESHING ALTERNATIVES TO THE TRADITIONAL RED AND GREEN.

MATERIALS:

• 4 purple magnolias with berry picks • 3 purple grape clusters • 4 glittered purple and green grape ivy stems with 3 trailers • 2 glittered twig branches • 2 14" (36cm) evergreen stems • 48" (1.2m) tall evergreen tree • Spanish moss • 10" x 8" (25cm x 20cm) iron and brass urn • white holiday lights (50 count) • 4 yards (4m) wired gold ribbon • 4 yards (4m) gold and white cording • gold spray paint • gold glitter spray • 2" (5cm) thick green floral sheet foam • greening pins • floral pick extenders • floral adhesive tape • green floral tape • 22–gauge floral wire • glue gun • wire cutters • hand trimmer

1: Prepare the Container

Using gold spray paint, lightly spray the Spanish moss with gold accents. When dry, fill the iron and brass urn with foam and cover it with the Spanish moss. Secure with greening pins.

2: Trim the Trunk

Use a hand trimmer to cut the trunk to 16" (41cm).

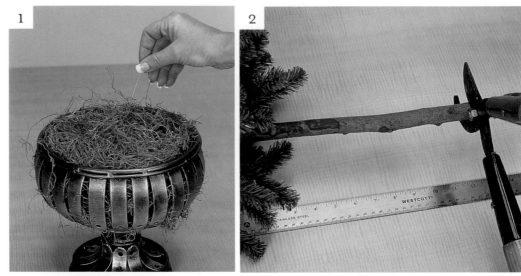

3: Insert and Secure the Tree into the Urn

Move the moss aside in the center of the container. Put glue on the bottom 2" (5cm) of the trunk and push it firmly into the foam. Push the moss back around the tree trunk. Open the tree up so it looks full and natural.

4: Add the Magnolias

Using three of the four magnolias in this step, place one magnolia to the right of center at the top of the tree. Place the second halfway down the tree to the left of center. Place the third toward the bottom—right side of the tree. Secure the magnolias by twisting the stems around the tree. If the stems are not long enough, secure with a glue gun.

5: ADD THE IVY TO THE TREE

*Cut two of the glittered grape ivy stems so that you have six 12"
(30cm) trailers. Place the stems throughout the tree where color
is needed and there are gaps between the magnolias. Set aside the
remaining two stems to be used in step 12.*

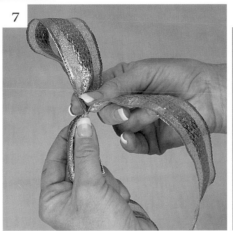

6: BEGIN THE BOWS

*Begin by making the cording bows to attach to the
gold bows. Use 1 yard (1m) for each bow and
make three loops. Fasten the bows together with
floral wire. Make a total of four cording bows, and
set them aside to be added to the gold bows.*

7: MAKE THE GOLD BOWS

*Pinch the ribbon between your finger approxi-
mately 4" (10cm) from the end of the ribbon. The
end piece of ribbon will become the first streamer
of the bow. Twist the ribbon with your fingers and
form a 9" (23cm) loop. Make another loop the
same size as the first loop, then twist. Repeat this
step until you have three loops of the same size.
Make a total of four of these gold bows.*

8: FASTEN THE BOWS TOGETHER

*Place a cording bow on top of each gold bow and
use the wires from the cording bow to fasten the
two together.*

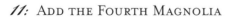

9: ADD THE BOWS AND RIBBONS TO THE TOPIARY

Place one bow at the top of the tree and fasten it with the wire from the bow. Cut off any excess wire. Weave ribbon and cording from the left of the tree down to the middle and right of the tree, using approximately 15" (38cm) of cording and ribbon. Place another bow in the middle of the topiary. Weave ribbon around the boughs and add a third bow at the base of the tree. Wrap more ribbon down the trunk. Place the final bow at the base of the urn, and secure it with a floral pick extender.

10: ADD THE EVERGREEN STEMS AND GRAPES

Insert the two evergreen stems to the left and right of the tree. Next, attach three grape clusters to floral pick extenders and insert them on the front left side of the urn.

11: ADD THE FOURTH MAGNOLIA

Add the fourth magnolia to the right of the trunk.

12: ADD THE GLITTERED IVY TRAILERS

Add the two glittered ivy stems you set aside in step 5. Cut these stems to 20" (51cm). Place one on either side of the tree with the evergreen stems. Stretch the two attached shorter trailers of the stem toward the front and back of the arrangement.

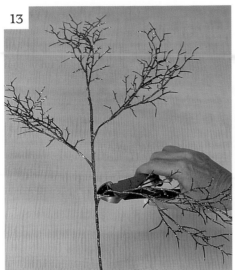

13

14

13: ADD THE TWIGS

Separate the glittered twig branches into small sprigs with 2" (5cm) stems and place them randomly throughout the tree and the arrangement.

14: ADD THE GLITTER & THE HOLIDAY LIGHTS

Spray the entire arrangement with gold glitter, then weave holiday lights through the tree.

DESIGNER **idea**

◆

For added sparkle

AND MAGIC DURING THE SEASON, ADD SMALL ORNAMENTS TO THE TREE. OR, YOU MAY WANT TO REPLACE THE MAGNOLIAS WITH FRUITS OR YOU MAY WANT TO MAKE AN ALL—ROSE TOPIARY. THIS PROJECT IS LOVELY, NOT ONLY FOR CHRISTMAS, BUT ALL YEAR ROUND.

St. Nicholas
Centerpiece

THIS SANTA WILL STEAL THE HEARTS OF ALL THOSE WHO BELIEVE. IT IS A STRIKING ONE—SIDED ARRANGEMENT THAT CAN BE USED ON A MANTEL OR ON A TABLE AGAINST A WALL. ALONG WITH WHITE MAGNOLIAS AND GOLD ACCENTS, THIS SANTA WILL REMIND YOU OF THE MAGIC OF CHRISTMAS AND ST. NICHOLAS.

MATERIALS:

• 2 20" (51cm) magnolias with buds • 4 evergreen stems • 4 English ivy trailers 12"–14" (30cm–36cm) long • 3 27" (69cm) gold wired curly twig stems • 1½ yards (1.5m) festive wired ribbon • Spanish moss • 11"x 8" (28cm x 20cm) gold ceramic container • Santa figurine approximately 12" (30cm) tall • gold spray paint • 2" (5cm) thick green floral sheet foam • greening pins • floral pick extenders • floral adhesive tape • wire cutters

1: PREPARE THE CONTAINER

Lightly spray the moss with gold spray paint. This particular pot is 3" (8cm) high, so I used two pieces of floral foam stacked together to fit inside the container. Then I cut a third piece of foam and placed it on top, securing it with floral adhesive. Cover the foam with the Spanish moss you sprayed gold, and secure it with greening pins.

2: ADD THE ST. NICK FIGURINE

Push aside the moss in the center and place St. Nick on top of the foam. Secure it with floral adhesive and press down firmly.

3: ADD THE EVERGREEN STEMS

Place two 12" (30cm) evergreen stems on the left and right sides of St. Nick. Place the third 12" (30cm) evergreen stem upward on the left side, next to St. Nick. Insert the 6" (15cm) stem in the right front side of the container.

tip

IF YOU HAVE DIFFICULTY LOCATING EVERGREEN STEMS, CONSIDER BUYING A SWAG. THERE ARE MANY REASONABLY PRICED SWAGS AVAILABLE IN STORES THAT ARE BEAUTIFULLY COLOR—COORDINATED. DON'T BE AFRAID CUT THEM APART AND USE THEM IN AN ARRANGEMENT.

4: Prepare the Magnolias

With wire cutters, snip apart the magnolia stems. Both the bud stems and the flower stems should be approximately 2" (5cm) long.

5: Add the Magnolias and Buds

Place one magnolia on the left front side lying on top of the greenery, and one on the right front side. Add the buds you trimmed off behind and slightly above each magnolia bloom.

6: Create Gold Accents

Snip off three 14" (36cm) ivy sprigs and one 12" (30cm). Create gold accents by lightly spraying them with gold spray paint.

7: Add the Ivy to the Arrangement

Place one 14" (36cm) ivy stem in the upper-left side of the figurine. Place two 14" (36cm) stems on either side of the Santa, and place the 12" (30cm) stem in the front, under the right magnolia.

8: Create a Bow

Following the bow-making techniques on pages 16–17, use 1½ yards (1.5m) of festive wired ribbon to create a four-loop bow with 6" (15cm) streamers.

9: Add the Bow to the Arrangement

Secure the bow with a floral pick, then insert it between the two magnolias, with one streamer flowing down to the right side and one up toward the left side.

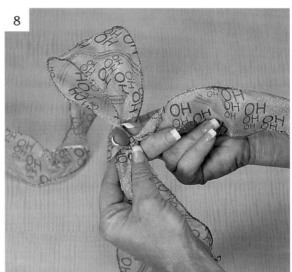

10: ADD THE GOLD CURLY BRANCHES

Place one 27" (69cm) gold curly branch upright, in front of the ivy on the left side of St. Nick. Insert two 24" (61cm) branches on either side of the magnolias. Place a 16" (41cm) branch within the green ivy in the front-right side of the arrangement.

DESIGNER idea

✦

Replace St. Nick

AND THE BOW WITH YOUR

FAVORITE CHRISTMAS FIGURINE

OR A SCENTED PILLAR CANDLE.

Winter Wonderland Wreath

CAPTURE THE BEAUTY OF WINTER WITH THIS EXQUISITE

WREATH. THE FROSTED WHITE ROSES AND IVY CREATE A STUNNING CONTRAST WITH

THE RED BOW AND BERRIES. ENJOY THIS ARRANGEMENT NOT ONLY DURING THE

HOLIDAYS, BUT THROUGHOUT THE FOLLOWING WINTER MONTHS AS WELL.

MATERIALS:

• 8 frosted white roses • 4 14" (36cm) evergreen stems • 2 frosted English ivy trailers • 3 extra–long berry branches • 20" (51cm) grapevine wreath • 3 3" (8cm) silver foam balls • 3½ yards (3.5m) red wired mesh ribbon • snow spray • 22–gauge floral wire • glue gun • wire cutters

1: ADD SNOW ACCENTS AND THE EVERGREEN STEMS

Lightly spray the wreath with snow spray paint to create snow accents. Then, trim three evergreen stems to 14" (36cm). Place two stems together at the top of the wreath. Glue the third stem to the bottom—right side of the wreath, draping downward.

2: CUT TWO EVERGREEN SPRIGS

Snip the fourth evergreen stem into two sprigs measuring 10" (25cm) long.

3: ADD THE EVERGREEN SPRIGS TO THE WREATH

Place one sprig at the top, between the two longer stems, growing up and out of the wreath. Insert another sprig in the bottom half of the wreath, just left of the pine stem draping downward. Secure both with a glue gun.

4: CREATE THE BOW

Leaving a 24" (61cm) streamer, make a loop using 13" (33cm) of ribbon. Twist the ribbon. Make another 13" (33cm) loop and twist. Repeat this until you have six loops of the same size. The remaining 24" (61cm) will be used as the other streamer. Secure the bow in the center with floral wire.

5: Add the Bow to the Wreath

Insert the bow in the center of the three evergreen stems. Use the floral wire in the center of the bow to fasten it to the wreath.

6: Attach the Streamers

Take two 6" (15cm) pieces of wire and attach the streamers to the lower—left and right sides of the wreath. Adjust the ribbon so the wires do not show.

7: Add the White Roses

Next, add the roses to the arrangement. Notice that the rose stems will get longer the farther away they are placed from the bow. Cut two 6" (15cm) rose stems and place one in the center of the bow, and the other on the evergreen stem in the lower-right side of the wreath. Cut two 8" (20cm) rose stems and insert them on either side of the large loops of the bow. Insert two 11" (28cm) stems under the blooms of the 8" (20cm) stems. Finally, place two 13" (33cm) stems under the blooms of the 11" (28cm) stems. Secure all the roses with a glue gun.

8: Snip the Frosted English Ivy Trailers

Cut one of the ivy sprigs from the stem, leaving two attached. Repeat this on both ivy stems.

9: Add the Ivy Trailers to the Wreath

Place the ivy stems with two vines attached under either side of the bow, hanging among the roses. Insert another ivy stem under the rose at the bottom of the wreath, and the third under the rose at the very top of the wreath. Secure the stems with a glue gun.

10: Add the Silver Balls

With a glue gun, attach the three silver balls to the wreath. Place one above the bow, the second below the bow, and glue the third onto the left streamer, on the lower-left side of the wreath.

11: INSERT THE BERRY STEMS

Place two berry stems at the top and on either side of the bow. Add the remaining berry stem at the lower-right side, flowing down from the wreath.

DESIGNER idea

✦

For Christmas,

YOU MAY WANT TO USE SPECIAL

ORNAMENTS IN PLACE OF THE

SILVER FOAM BALLS.

Classic Evergreen Wreath

THIS TRADITIONAL WREATH IS AN INVITING SIGHT ON YOUR FRONT DOOR, WELCOMING FAMILY AND FRIENDS DURING THE HOLIDAY SEASON. EVERGREENS AND RED POINSETTIAS—THE TRADITIONAL FOLIAGE OF CHRISTMAS— NEVER GO OUT OF STYLE. THE GOLD HYDRANGEAS, BERRIES AND RIBBON ACCENT AN ALREADY STUNNING WREATH TO GIVE IT A DRAMATIC AND UNIQUE LOOK.

103

MATERIALS:

• *3 large poinsettias with gold—dipped edges* • *3 glittered hydrangeas* • *6 12"* *(30cm) gold berry stems* • *1 stem of glittered and flocked grape ivy trailers* • *1 30" (76cm) evergreen wreath* • *white holiday lights (35 count)* • *5 yards (5m) gold wired ribbon* • *glitter spray paint* • *floral pick extenders* • *glue gun* • *wire cutters*

1: OPEN THE WREATH

*When you purchase a wreath, it usually comes smashed and flat.
Open the wreath up by stretching some pine stems to the side and
some straight up so it looks full and natural.*

2: SEPARATE AND ADD THE GRAPE IVY

*Cut three ivy trailers from the stem. Place the ivy around the inner
circle of the wreath and secure it with a glue gun.*

3

3: Add the Poinsettias

Cut the poinsettia stems to 6" (15cm) and place them proportionally around the wreath. Use a glue gun to secure the stems to the wreath.

4: Add the Hydrangeas & Gold Berries

Cut the three hydrangea stems to 6" (15cm) and place them proportionally around the poinsettias. Use a glue gun to secure the stems. Cut the six gold berry stems to 12" (30cm) and insert one on each side of the poinsettias, pointing outward from the wreath.

5: Make the Bows

Begin the first bow by pinching the ribbon between your fingers approximately 10" (25cm) from the end of the ribbon. The end piece of the ribbon will become the first streamer of the bow. Twist the ribbon with your fingers and form a small loop, using 12" (30cm) of ribbon for the loop. Make another loop the same size as the first. Secure the bow by wrapping the loops together with floral wire in the center. Repeat this step to make two more bows.

4

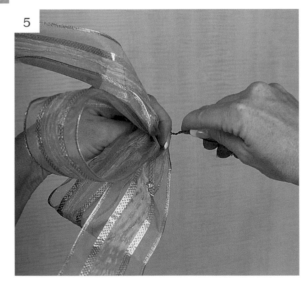

5

6: ADD THE BOWS TO THE WREATH

Insert the bows underneath the poinsettias. Use floral wire in the center of the bows to fasten them to the wreath. Trim the ends of the streamers with a diagonal cut to the desired length.

7: ADD STREAMERS THROUGHOUT THE WREATH

Weave the remaining ribbon throughout the wreath, between the hydrangeas, poinsettias and the bows. Secure the ribbon with evergreen boughs where necessary.

8: ADD FINAL TOUCHES

Spray the entire wreath with gold glitter spray. Add a strand of white holiday lights for a festive look.

DESIGNER **idea**

✦

Feature magnolias

AFTER THE CHRISTMAS HOLIDAY

IN PLACE OF POINSETTIAS

FOR THE REMAINING

WINTER MONTHS.

Christmas Holiday Swag

TRY THIS UNIQUE ALTERNATIVE IN PLACE OF A WREATH FOR THE CHRISTMAS SEASON. THIS SWAG NOT ONLY LOOKS GREAT ON A DOOR, BUT IT CAN BE USED ON A WALL WHERE A TOUCH OF ELEGANCE IS NEEDED. IT IS A VERY VERSATILE PIECE, AND WILL ADD A FESTIVE TOUCH TO ANY ROOM.

MATERIALS:

• *1 36" (91cm) evergreen wall swag* • *1 36" (91cm) magnolia with berries swag* • *3 yards (3m) festive wired ribbon* • *2 wired twig branches* • *22–gauge floral wire* • *glue gun* • *wire cutters*

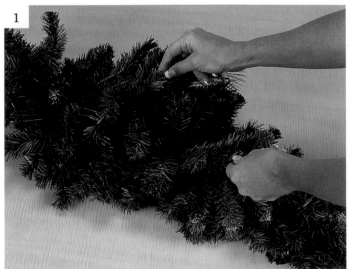

1: Open the Evergreen Swag

When you purchase an evergreen swag it is usually flat and smashed. Open the swag up by stretching some pine stems to the side and some straight up so it looks full and natural.

2: Add the Magnolia Swag

Place the magnolia swag on top of the evergreen swag, and secure it by twisting evergreen branches around the magnolia swag in several places.

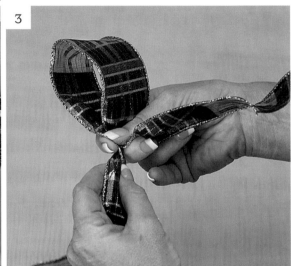

3: Create Bow Tucks

A bow tuck is simply a bow that has only a few loops. It is looser than a formal bow. Begin by pinching the ribbon between your fingers approximately 6" (15cm) from the end of the ribbon. The end piece of ribbon will become the first streamer of the bow tuck. Twist the ribbon with your fingers and form a small loop, using 12" (30cm) for the loop. Make two more loops, and remember to twist the ribbon after you make each loop. Secure the bow in the center with a piece of floral wire.

4: Add a Bow Tuck to the Swag

Starting at the top of the swag, place the bow tuck under the top magnolia. Use the floral wire in the center of the bow tuck to secure it to the swag.

5: Add Another Bow Tuck

Bring the ribbon down the swag through the pine boughs to the next set of magnolias. Add another bow tuck as instructed in step 3, making just two loops.

6: Add the Final Bow Tuck

Continue to bring the ribbon down to the bottom magnolia. Add another bow tuck as instructed in step 3, making just one loop with the end of the ribbon hanging down. Trim the ribbon to 6" (15cm). Place the bow under the bottom magnolia.

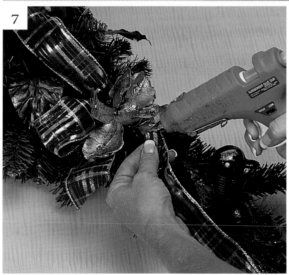

7: Add Streamers

Cut 10" (25cm) of the remaining ribbon for a final streamer. Fold the ribbon in half and glue it under the bow. You should now have two streamers hanging from the bottom of the swag.

8: SEPARATE THE TWIG BRANCHES

Cut apart the twig branches to make four bunches, each approximately 12" (30cm) long.

9: ADD THE BRANCHES TO THE SWAG

Place one branch at the top, angled to the right. Place another branch in the upper—left side of the swag. Insert the third branch in the lower—right part of the swag, and place the final one at the bottom, angled to the left.

DESIGNER **idea**

◆

For a classic look,

REPLACE THE MAGNOLIAS WITH

RED POINSETTIAS DURING THE

CHRISTMAS SEASON.

Christmas Garland

CREATE THIS CHRISTMAS GARLAND TO COMPLEMENT THE

TRADITIONAL WREATH OR THE CHRISTMAS HOLIDAY SWAG.

WEAVE THE EVERGREEN GARLAND THROUGH THE HANDRAIL OF

YOUR STAIRCASE, AROUND A DOORWAY, ACROSS YOUR MANTEL OR

ANYWHERE ELSE THAT YOU WANT TO ADD A WARM, FESTIVE FEEL

TO YOUR HOLIDAY DÉCOR.

Make this garland by creating three separate swags and attaching them to the evergreen garland.

1. *To make one swag, fasten a grape ivy trailer to a bunch of gold berries and a gold twig with floral tape.*

2. *Cut the stems to 4" (10cm).*

3. *Add a red poinsettia to the bundle.*

4. *Make another ivy, berry and twig bundle, leaving 4" (10cm) stems; bind with floral tape.*

5. *Place the two bundles together with the berries facing outward and the poinsettia in the center. Bind the two together with floral tape.*

6. *Next, make two bows, one with 2 yards (2m) plaid wired ribbon and one with 2½ yards (2.5m) gold wired ribbon.*

7. *With the plaid ribbon, make two 12" (30cm) loops with two 18" (43cm) streamers.*

8. *With the gold ribbon, make two 15" (38cm) loops and two 18" (43cm) streamers.*

9. *Fasten the bows together with floral wire, plaid bow on top; then add the bow to the swag.*

10. *After you have made three swags, attach them proportionately to the garland, beginning 24" (61cm) from the garland's end.*

11. *Add four glittered hydrangeas, then weave 5 yards (5m) of gold wired ribbon through the garland.*

12. *Spray with glitter spray and add white holiday lights for a final touch.*

Christmas Ornament Arrangement

THIS SIMPLE YET ELEGANT

ARRANGEMENT WILL ADD CHARM AND SOPHISTICATION TO YOUR HOLIDAY DÉCOR.

THE GOLD AND BURGUNDY, ACCOMPANIED BY DARK EVERGREEN STEMS, MAKE THIS

ARRANGEMENT A LOVELY PIECE ON A DINING ROOM TABLE.

MATERIALS:

• *3 large glittered white poinsettias* • *2 9" (23cm) ornaments of your choice*
• *4 14" (36cm) evergreen stems* • *3 16" (41cm) burgundy eucalyptus berry*
stems • *1 glittered gold French grape bush* • *4 30" (76cm) gold curly twig*
branches • *Spanish moss* • *10" (25cm) diameter brass container* • *2" (5cm)*
thick green floral sheet foam • *greening pins* • *floral pick extenders* • *floral*
adhesive tape • *green floral tape* • *glue gun* • *wire cutters*

1: PREPARE THE CONTAINER

Stack three pieces of floral foam and attach them securely to the container with floral adhesive tape and greening pins. Cover the foam with Spanish moss, and secure it with greening pins.

2: ADD TWO EVERGREEN STEMS

Insert one 14" (36cm) evergreen stem on each side of the container.

3: SEPARATE THE REMAINING EVERGREEN STEMS

Cut the two remaining evergreen stems so that you have four 12" (30cm) sprigs.

4: INSERT THE EVERGREEN SPRIGS

Insert two sprigs upright in the center of the foam, one pointing to the front and the other angled toward the back. Insert the third sprig in the front and the final sprig in the back.

5: ADD THE EUCALYPTUS BERRY STEMS

Attach each berry stem to a floral pick. Place the stems between the evergreens. Insert them at a downward angle so they hang over the edge of the container.

6: ADD THE POINSETTIAS

Cut the poinsettias to 9" (23cm). Place them proportionally around the center of the container, just above the berries and greenery.

7: INSERT THE GOLD TWIGS

Cut each stem of gold twigs to 24" (61cm), saving
the remainder of the stems to be used in step 8.
Insert the twigs in the center of the arrangement.

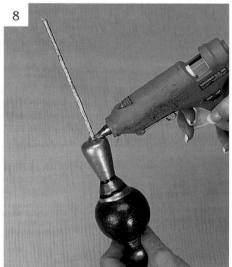

8: PREPARE THE ORNAMENTS

Remove the hangers from the ornaments with your wire cutters.
Using the 6" (15cm) stems cut off from the gold twigs in step 7,
glue a twig into each ornament.

9: INSERT THE ORNAMENTS
INTO THE ARRANGEMENT

Insert the ornaments just to the left and right of the gold twigs,
inserting one slightly deeper in the foam than the other.

10: ADD THE GLITTERED GOLD FRENCH GRAPE GREENERY

Snip the glittered gold French grape greenery into separate stems. Place the longer stems of greenery around the bottom of the arrangement, between the eucalyptus berry stems. Place the shorter stems around the gold twigs and the poinsettia, filling in where needed.

DESIGNER idea

◆

To create

A UNIQUE ARRANGEMENT

EACH YEAR, REPLACE THE TWO

ORNAMENTS WITH NEW ONES.

ORNAMENTS FROM PAST YEARS

CAN BE DISPLAYED ON YOUR

CHRISTMAS TREE.

Sleigh & Candle Centerpiece

CREATE A FESTIVE YET SOPHISTICATED PIECE WITH EVERGREEN STEMS, GOLD BERRIES AND POINSETTIAS. INSTEAD OF A TRADITIONAL VASE, THIS UNIQUE ARRANGEMENT IS CONSTRUCTED ON A MINIATURE SLEIGH. IT MAKES A CHARMING CENTERPIECE FOR A DINNER PARTY OR A BEAUTIFUL ADORNMENT ON A COFFEE TABLE WHEN ENTERTAINING FAMILY AND FRIENDS.

MATERIALS:

• 2 large blue poinsettias • 2 gold grape cluster stems • 2 gold and silver plastic pears • 2 18" (46cm) evergreen stems • Spanish moss • 20" x 7" (51cm x 18cm) sleigh • 9" (23cm) square pillar candle • 3 yards (3m) gold wired ribbon • 2" (5cm) thick green floral sheet foam • greening pins • floral pick extenders • floral adhesive tape • green floral tape • glue gun • wire cutters • paring knife

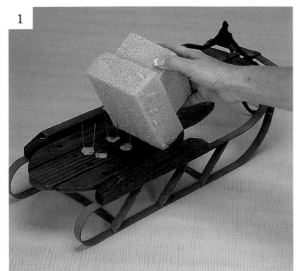

1: Prepare the Sleigh with Foam

Cut a 3" x 6" (8cm x 15cm) piece of foam and attach it to the sleigh using greening pins and floral adhesive. Cut another piece of foam the width of the candle and stack it on top of the first, securing it with floral adhesive.

2: Add the Moss

Cover the foam with moss and secure it with greening pins, leaving the center of the foam free of moss so the candle can rest directly on the foam.

3: Add the Pillar Candle

Add floral adhesive to the bottom of the candle and place the candle on top of the foam. Press down firmly.

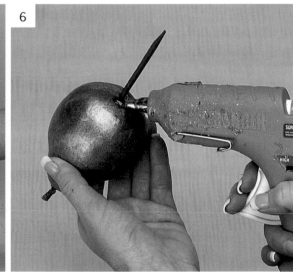

4: ADD THE EVERGREEN

Cut the evergreen stems to 18" (46cm). Insert one stem diagonally towards the back left and one diagonally to the front right.

5: ADD THE POINSETTIAS

Cut each poinsettia stem to 4" (10cm). Insert one poinsettia in the front left corner and one in the back right corner, with the extra leaves inserted in a cluster below the poinsettias. The leaves may have to be to attached to floral pick extenders for extra strength.

6: PREPARE THE PEARS

Poke a small hole in each pear with a paring knife. Cut the wires off of two floral picks. Glue the floral pick extenders inside the holes with a glue gun.

7: Insert the Pears into the Arrangement

Insert one pear to the left of each poinsettia.

8: Add the Grape Clusters

Cut the grape cluster stems to 14" (36cm) and insert within the greenery.

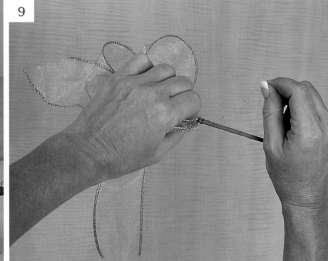

9: Make the Bows

For this project you will need two bows. Cut the 3 yards (3m) of ribbon in half. Begin the bow by pinching the ribbon between your fingers approximately 12"(30cm) from the end of the ribbon. The end piece of ribbon will become the first streamer of the bow. Twist the ribbon with your fingers and form a small loop using another 11" (28cm) of the ribbon. Make two more loops of the same size, twisting the ribbon between each loop and leaving a 12" (30cm) piece of ribbon for the other streamer. Repeat this step to make the second bow.

10: ADD THE BOWS
TO THE ARRANGEMENT

Fasten the bows to floral pick extenders.
Insert the bows next to the candle.

DESIGNER idea

✦

Complement the

DECOR IN YOUR HOME

BY CHOOSING APPROPRIATE

COLORS. POINSETTIAS ARE

AVAILABLE IN A WIDE RANGE OF

COLORS AND STYLES,

SO PICK ONES THAT SUIT

YOUR TASTE.

BEVERLY'S CRAFTS & FABRICS

100 COTTON LANE
SOQUEL, CA 95073
toll free: 1-877-308-5858
e-mail: FH@beverly.com

www.save-on-crafts.com/welcome.html

• *Florals, floral supplies, ribbons, vases, Christmas store*

C.M. OFFRAY & SON, INC.

360 ROUTE 24
CHESTER, NJ 07930
tel: (800) 551-LION

www.offray.com

• *Decorative ribbons*

DESIGN MASTER COLOR TOOL, INC.

P.O. BOX 601
BOULDER, CO 80306
tel: (303) 443-5214
fax: (303) 443-5217

www.dmcolor.com

• *Floral scents, floral color sprays, paints and tints*

FLORACRAFT

ONE LONGFELLOW PLACE
P.O. BOX 400
LUDINGTON, MI 49431
tel: (616) 843-0240

www.floracraft.com

• *Floral sheet foam and general floral supplies*

FLOWERS BY DESIGN

470 MISSION ST. UNIT #11
CAROL STREAM, IL 60188
tel: (630) 665-9333
toll free: 1-800-833-SILK
fax: (630) 665-9390

www.flowers-b-design.com

• *High-end silk flowers, berries, foliage, fruits and vegetables, containers, ribbons, accessories, floral supplies (Wholesale distributor, no minimum order)*

OASIS FLORAL PRODUCTS

P.O. BOX 118
KENT, OH 44240
tel: (800) 321-8286
fax: (800) 447-0813

www.smitheroasis.com

• *Floral foam products*

SANTA'S SUPPLY

N 9678 N. SUMMIT LANE
SUMMIT LAKE, WI 54485
tel: (715) 275-4188
fax: (715) 275-5052
e-mail: rbjeske@newnorth.net

www.santasupplies.com

• *Silk floral products, ribbon, wreath rings, assorted wreath picks, pre-made bows ($50 minimum order)*

SILK 'N SUE LTD.

UNIT 1 LAGOON ROAD
CRAY AVENUE
ORPINGTON
KENT BR5 3QX
UK
tel: 01 689 823 293
fax: 01 689 877 872
e-mail: info@silknsue.co.uk

www.silknsue.co.uk

• *Artificial plants, trees, flowers, Christmas showroom*

SILKS & WEDDING SUPPLIES

N 9678 N. SUMMIT LANE
SUMMIT LAKE, WI 54485
tel: (715) 275-4188
toll free: 1-800-772-6827
fax: (715) 275-5052
e-mail: rbjeske@newnorth.net

www.silks-weddingsupplies.com/silkflorals.html

• *Silk flowers and greenery, silk floral products*

W. J. Cowee, Inc.

28 TAYLOR AVE.
P.O. BOX 248
BERLIN, NY 12022
tel: (800) 658-2233
fax: (518) 658-2244

www.cowee.com

• *Floral picks and general floral supplies*

Create gorgeous floral gifts and décor
WITH NORTH LIGHT BOOKS!

Whether planning a grand Thanksgiving dinner, a tropical theme party for friends, or a romantic dinner for two, you'll find a wealth of creative silk and dried floral projects inside. Learn how to select the right flowers, create each arrangement step-by-step and enhance any table setting with floral accents. The results are simply magnificent! 1-55870-598-8, paperback, 128 pages, #70537-K

Capture the essence of the seasons with these simple, stunning floral arrangements. With a few basic techniques, a handful of materials, and a little creativity, you can make eye-pleasing accents for every room in your home. All the flower arranging advice you need is inside, plus 15 projects using silk flowers, greenery, leaves, pinecones, gourds and more. 1-58180-108-4, paperback, 96 pages, #31810-K

Here are 20 beautiful wreath projects, perfect for brightening up a doorway or celebrating a special time of year. You'll find a range of sizes and styles, utilizing a variety of creative materials, including dried herbs, sea shells, cinnamon sticks, silk flowers, Autumn leaves, Christmas candy and more. Clear, step-by-step instructions ensure beautiful, long lasting results every time! 1-58180-239-0, paperback, 144 pages, #32015-K

Whether you're the bride-to-be, a member of the wedding party, or a close friend, this book can show you how to create gorgeous floral arrangements for priceless wedding memories. You'll find guidelines for crafting 20 step-by-step projects, from the bride's bouquet and boutonnieres to pew decorations and wedding cake toppers. 1-55870-560-0, paperback, 128 pages, #70488-K